GW00806421

# salmonpoetry

*Publishing Irish & International
Poetry Since 1981*

# The Egret Lands With News from Other Parts

Mary Madec

Published in 2019 by

Salmon Poetry

Cliffs of Moher, County Clare, Ireland

www.salmonpoetry.com  e: info@salmonpoetry.com

ISBN 978-1-912561-67-4

Cover & Internal Images: *Breda Burns – www.bredaburns.com*
Cover Design & Typesetting: *Siobhán Hutson*
*Printed in Ireland by Sprint Print*

*Salmon Poetry gratefully acknowledges the support of*
*The Arts Council / An Chomhairle Ealaíon*

*for Conall*

# Contents

*One*

# The Egret Lands with News from Other Parts

I wish it were to a place
emptied of memories

not caught in the gauze of those thin trees
on the banks of a river which heaves
until I'm up to my knees in its detritus.

The hill above, which I have walked
so many times, leaves me once again breathless
at the summit, as if it were the wrong road.

What I didn't know then
hops out like a harlequin from behind the hedges,
mocks me on those lonely walks

the smell of gorse or woodbine in my nose
where I thought a sweet scented world was consoling me,
not telling me I'd make better memories somewhere else

in another world, from where the egret came,
his cascade of white plumes flowing down as he stoops
and dallies in the inlet long enough for me to notice him

then raises to the span
of his brilliant majestic wings,
the grey world receding, colour seeping through.

# Redaction in the Inlet

Lick out the rawness and deceit,
find the truth that hides beneath

the dead centre, that place of ignominy
from which you cry out of your animal self,

maybe it's a soul, if that's not too much of a word
drawn from an old creed no one believes in.

Claim it before love dies, before
you stare back into the black hole

from which you know you must have come
repeating as you work out in this poem

how the wound flies in the face of logic,
gives you goals for your high art indeed

consolation from the lick, like a dog's kiss
nuzzles your egomaniacal sadness

staying with the crazy mystery
of good agony, how it re-appropriates history

which you'll sort by the laws of parsimony
the extravagance of idiolect.

# The Burden of History

I'd like to walk upon the earth without trampling on the history of my kin,
so many roads are famine walks

and underneath the wild strawberry
powdered bones in the ditches.

Behind grammatical mysteries like why John Hill's was not John's hill,
a story of lives lost in time and struggles that came to nothing.

The Cillín in the middle of the farm and some mother now long forgotten
who stood over it weeping

and, in that inlet of my ancestors where I stood in awe of the cottage garden
a girl looks back, witnesses a young woman raped by a neighbour.

These booby traps in the ground on the ready to detonate—
and every step I take, an expiation

even if one is no more guilty than being alive, and being alive, in danger
of remembering in one's bones too much sorrow.

# Civil War

Your delicate rushing towards freedom
of writing in the small hours

the attrition of words, their solace
as you knead them with the fists

of your inner strife, lonely and celibate.
No hope you think of being a wife

to anyone but this. This adulterous world
with no respect for the price

of freedom. No idea of what it's worth
coaxing you to fatuous compromises.

Better not to come out all guns
on the foolishness of the superficial life.

Who cares how one's coiffe is done
or how well the bustle fits to drape

the gaze from neck to waist. You are looking out
now at the first light of day

which penetrates right into your aching bones
as the ink dries. That little bird of hope

ruffles under your bodice and you hold it
so tenderly before you release it to morning.

You have fought to daybreak,
lament how your brother went south.

You lose the battles one by one, contumely, the other cheek
until you fall like all mortals

the battles lost, the war won.

# This is the Place We Enter the River

where water flows deep and calm on New Year's Eve.
Later, as Spring comes, we will watch
for salmon leap, crêpe de Chine on trees.
Warm in the ice-house we dream human dreams
of how new life is made from all that has been
which the river holds, as you do me.

Through the silence of night the trees
drop heavy blobs onto the Velux
which roll slowly down the roof
like beads of hematite
until the first timid light
of the New Year makes them translucent.

You go downstairs, bring back a flask of tea
and we sit up and sip the dark liquid
as if it were a healing potion
to make everything alright,
our half-formed thoughts
disappearing with wisps of steam.

Now, we are in the river, down in the riverbed
where the pearl of great price
glistens like a salmon's eye
waiting for us to find that love is deeper still
like a bedrock we might never reach
in this lifetime.

# The Pink Dancing Costume

*for Medbh McGuckian*


I fill the tracings of the dragon with stem stitch, the silk threads
lined up in every inch of his long body, laid out on the great circle
of my bishop's pink serge, with its black satin lining, its fine crochet,
white rose collar and cuffs. I work steadily with my mother

until it is done and I stand in front of her as if to walk upon the stage,
the light jumping on the silken threads, my feet pointed until the pounce
at the start of the music, turns and twirls and rocks in the dance
of the nation, the magic of my feet, the pride and elation of our handiwork:

*One two three four, one two three four, one two three four, up and down*
*One two three four, one two three four, one two three four, up and down*
*Hop to three four, cross two three four, one tip one, rock two three,*
*Hop to three four, cross two three four, one tip one, rock two three....*

# Primer

I have moved at last into the third person
where I am able to forgive on principle
at a comfortable distance

how you left me like a dangling infinitive
looking for a sentence
settling my ear to the music of words
to integrate the absurd

rhythms to tap out in the darkness
from memories in the present subjunctive,
*amem, ames, amet*

my mnemonic, the distant chimneys of a house
in Fr. Angelus Park.
*That I, you, he, she, may love*
in a perfect world.

The conditional seems more predictable
though I cannot see all the conditions that might pertain
or the rules for their use after certain clauses.

Even if I know all the rules of the grammar
I stumble on composing the narrative
hesitate to make the bold interpretation of an unknown world
*Gallia est omnis partes tres divisa est.*

When I get to the Rubicon, I struggle with retrospect
settle on the third person
for space between me and the world.

# Imagine

After *The Wife's Lament* from *The Exeter Book*

They banished me from the scriptorium
as if only Caedmon could wake to a dream.
They treated me like a mute bondswoman
yet I can say exactly how I was feeling in that earth cave.
I can retrieve every detail so you can feel the briars that tore me
           the smack of the waves on the shore
the scent of a storm in the breeze
as I hide in the shade of the oak leaves
and sometimes at my deepest heartbreak
I ask myself was it worth the trouble
my efforts to reach you?
I ask myself was it worth the trouble,
and sometimes at my deepest heartbreak
as I hide in the shade of the oak leaves
the scent of a storm in the breeze
           the smack of the waves on the shore
I can retrieve every detail so you can feel the briars that tore me
I can say exactly how I was feeling in that earth cave
yet they treated me like a mute bondswoman
as if only Caedmon could wake to a dream
they banished me from the scriptorium.

*Two*

# The Green Room

We, the women, come and go
not one common lingo between us

as we sit, sip tea or coke
too self-absorbed trying to do the crossword
before our turn to walk out into the limelight,

the old fears at us, as if we are back in the classroom
pitched against each other
wondering who has the sweetest voice.

We were, are, never in the boys' club
though some of us are lifted up like oracles
for our prophecies, the aptness of our words.

Here we are polite, deferent, as at a *Poetry Ireland Introductions*.
We stretch our fingers to take Boland's biscuits from a plate
with a doily in the centre of the table, savour the delicate taste.

We think of the clues: One dreams of a horse with a mane sent
from across the bitter sea looking in over the half door
at the cream crawling up the jug.

An office girl rubs Lincoln creams from her mouth
counts pages offshore, longing for the boat
back to Dún Laoghaire.

In Galway, an abandoned nest keeps its place in an old ruin
miles from Donegal, a silk road wends its way to a sea wall
where a woman plunges a knife in the wave.

Somewhere in Belfast a young mother looks through a window
over Strangford Lough and an older woman
searches for patchwork pieces on the internet

and all over the island the interpolation of Greek lament in timid voices
of the lineage. I am checking out words in the Dictionary of Obscure
Sorrows, finding one word that fits all,

monochopsis, *the subtle but persistent feeling of being maladapted,*
for example, a selkie on a beach — *lumbering, clumsy,*
*easily distracted* but pretending not to be

*huddled in the company of other misfits,* you recognise this
your voice one scale at least above *the ambient roar*
*of your intended habitat*

*in which you'd be fluidly, brilliantly, effortlessly at home,*
if only they would listen. Get them to listen, all of them
you tell yourself, as you make your way from the Green Room.

# First Reading

It was not exactly a school of thought
at least, not first, when I polished my words
and went on the stage.

I appreciated the hush of my fellow citizens
and my sister women. I knew some of them
at least would understand what I was saying,

how I choked on the backstory but held out
for the glint of the razor sharp turns of phrase,
the anger underneath, mine and maybe theirs,

sometimes despair that nothing would change.
Afterwards a bouquet. Were they carnations or lilies?
He pressed them into my fists,
the supplication drowned by the applause.

# For Every Tatter in Her Mortal Dress

Will you tell the *Cailleach Bhéara*, the Queen of Winter
whose rumpled hands hang limply by her side,
whose scabby shins lie bare, vulnerable at the end of her thin dress,
will you tell her that she doesn't count because she is old?
Because she is no longer beautiful to you
the self appointed judge, though her fine mind on fire
is enough to light up these dark ages.

Will you tell her that only the minds of old women
are forgotten, remain nothing, are smudged
out of the annals? A more paltry thing
than the tattered mortal man whose song
beats upon the ballast of Byzantium?

Take care what you say to her, daughter,
and remember what brought her to this precipice.
Her song will find its words in the wind and the rain
and the hum of the summer breeze,
the howl of the banshee when she comes.
Lead her gently back, this greying *cailleach*
to a resting place in the green hills of hope
beyond the *mutinous Shannon* and the *sraith salach*
beyond the Pale.

*Cailleach Bhéara* (Irish/Gaelic) – old woman of Beara, the Goddess of Winter
*Sraith salach* (Irish/Gaelic) – dark marsh

# Her Time Has Come to Go Under the Bridge

*After a story told by an Irish Traveller, Newcastle West, Ireland. Field notes, 1983*

The crows squall out of the trees from her cries,
        the bridge above her mirrors the arc of her legs.
Rodents smell blood from the water, wait in the undergrowth
        for the afterbirth, do not dare for now
with respect for the living, with deference for this mammalian state
        to devour what is just about to be born.
The girl rises from the waters like the Virgin of the Apocalypse
        the remnant of her seed,
a healthy baby opens wide his purple lips and screams,
        inhales his first mouthful of air.
She cuts the chord and waits until the big mushroom of blood falls into the water,
        before she makes her way with the baby back to the camp,
swings him over the water's flow as instructed
        in the name of the Father, Son and Holy Ghost.
She picks her way back over the fields, trips on twigs and stones
        and yet gets home as if two wings of a great eagle
had taken her, body and bones, into the arms of the midwives, the older women
        waiting with stanching bandages and swaddling.
The men cannot bear to think of that dark hole from which the baby came,
        they fear the miracle, they fear the girl,
deem her unclean, say she has to stay out of sight
        to keep the camp safe, until the forces are appeased.
Even the one who believes it was his seed, believes he was part of it,
        agrees she is dangerous now, mysterious.
She learns this truth at sixteen, her breasts stiff as melons for suckle
        hidden from the men who say she is untouchable
in the post partum wilderness of rawness and sore nipples
        and though she is hungry, she must not prepare food for forty days,
there would be no strength in it.  She must fast
        until the globe of her abdomen contracts
to their world, until the forces which turned her insides out, subside.
        The midwives agree to inspect the lochia
and they all count the days, parrying with nature, fate,
all glad that the baby is alive, glad and terrified.

# Subject

A Persephone blurred in your mirror
before you offered the pomegranate in error.

I saw the old knife on the table, guessed
with such a blunt instrument, you'd make a terrible mess,

scatter all those seeds like tiny garnets,
unleash some power you wanted in fact to harness.

Or was I Demeter, you aware of me usefully there
for errands, an emissary to bear gifts to others

and go to places where you wouldn't
waste your graces?

I have found a pillar against the moon
which gives no shelter in the dark

but I can stay in the shadows
work out how despots rule.

I am like an old rug
you bought to cover a broken floorboard,

some old jug which pours better
than the milk carton,

some old sofa you sat on without thanking it
for its support, its scatter cushions.

I come to be the bane of your existence
a discomfiting likeness, in me you see your nemesis.

Sure I could learn to forgive how you looked
through me to everyone else, choked

that I was some strange test
because I was closer than all the rest,

so close I didn't exist
in the true meaning of the word.

At the end of the garden where the narcissi grow higher
than anywhere else, you blew your trumpet.

I see the door of a marble hall up ahead,
its copper handle shiny and red

like ribbons of sunset which fell from the sky
in its vastness, the omens of clouds.

My loneliness soars so high.

# My Empty Nest

Through an open window a cuckoo sings in the night, full-throated notes
distend her bellows
        ricochet into the mildness of May.

I think wryly of my emptying nest, then in cuckoo land pace myself
for obsequies where I walk uphill
        push though briars, looking back for my breast-craving babies

I toss and turn, find myself young, nubile, before they came, drowned
in the *Exeter Book's* cuckoo call in the bitter exiles
        of *The Wanderer, The Seafarer, The Wife's Lament.*

Something's upstaged in me, the crook of my arms undone, the sound
of the bird's call pushing me in rage
        out of my own earth cave.

The cuckoo says, *It is yours no more.*
        *No more for you the comfort of tried and true.*

*If I didn't push you, you'd miss*
        *the new life which is searching for you.*

It doesn't make sense for me to fly into the crosswinds, I protest.
        *Fly you must.*

*Nothing you've had by way of skill will prove useful again,*
        *your nestlings have flown.*

I wonder what I need to do with no nest to make
        this, my problem through the night

obsessing about it until I wake and weep inconsolably for my lost babies,
        my emptiness.

Three

# The Past Still Barks at Me

*I*

On the morning he comes through the gate
I see the wound is still there,

hope it is not too late for him to be healed.

I know he has sailed three sheets to the wind
into every port he thought might be his destiny,
one-eyed insights and sirens holding him custody.


*II*

I'd like to say I forgive you.
I took my time coming near.
I needed to know you still

recalled the secret of our chamber.

Did you guess I'd use it as a test?
It's now a leafy canopy,
I need to know if you can remember yet

not the dog, but your old olive tree,

if you can love its gnarled branches,
my hands searching for your face
somewhere in the in-between of sleep,

tracing out your lips, feeling the grade one sandpaper of your cheek

your pulling me closer as if
you were protecting me from bad dreams,
a delicate hurry for confirmation

this is real beyond the milky eyes of morning.

# The Window

I just can't clean it, can't see through.
It did not begin like this. It was once a good house, a good window.
I remember the gleam, the glass brand new,
my reflection, and you, playfully pressing your lips
on the glass, pretending to kiss me.

It's not just the streaks after a perfect wipe which light reveals as imperfect.
You do not seem to see me clearly nor I you. I want to clean the pane,
rinse the in-between, but I look at you through the dirty glass
and I know that my gaze is strange and merciless, what I see in your gaze too
as if I am someone you never knew.

Of course we should be glad of the stream of light
on this Spring morning making a path along the floor.
Your eyes are searching for something more
beyond me, as if I have become an antique dresser
in an old room with which you were once familiar.

What is it about the way your arms hang awkwardly?
You look like a prisoner, and you have something
to say about how intolerable dirty windows are.
Then I see that what you are staring at
is not the window but the door.

# Fragile

I stand in the kitchen saying goodbye to the house

I have lived in, mother and lover

when I see a song thrush, dead at the door of the sun lounge

stunned forever by the clarity of glass.

I look at his small frail body, his speckled chest

but most of all at his two spindle legs limply clinging to air

as if there could be something they could grab

to stop the folding of this fragile life back into the earth.

# Bangs

I look at myself in the mirror.
*Mmm ... Nice,* I think. *Updates me,* I say to the hairdresser, laughing
then rush outside to the car where my husband is waiting.

He says nothing at first until I ask, *Well, what do you think?*
He says he doesn't recognise me
not that he wouldn't recognise me.

Back at home, I stand at the mirror *Am I that different?*
I begin to see a foreign body looking out at me,
blurring as I stare.

I grow fragile from this perception
embarrassed by the sexy sweep to the side,
girlie bangs in my eyes.

I tell myself I don't care
what he thinks, but all evening I wait for the manly lines of a smile
so I can retreat to the one I was before.

I brace myself, wait for more of me
to come back to him, imagine
he'll say, *actually you look alluring!*

I shrink behind my fringe, return his deadpan glance.
I become the woman with the new haircut who was never seen
again by her husband, who walked into the mirror and shattered it.

# For Something to Say

You tell me about the Crimean war,
sharing a book you've read

to fill this painful silence between us,
to bind the wounds of an argument.

It's serious but I'm amused and wonder if you realise
it's famous for logistical and technical errors.

I say nothing. I know we should compromise
not go down the war path. I want to say something

and imagine trenches out of which we cannot dig
ourselves,

the valley of death into which Tennyson's
six hundred rode.

You are trying to explain how thoughts are contagious,
the power of the collective unconscious

how once unleashed evil takes hold
and strangles all that we know of goodness.

The Sisters of Mercy, who went to care
for the wounded, ignored.

Still no words come. I pull at fragile seams between us
to see what's seething underneath

the dust of battlefields.
I want to run for cover,

quit my post. Far away, war cries,
shells detonate, ricochet into dark

thoughts. I'm lost for words.
I hold my hand out for yours.

All a minefield.

# Three Decades Between Myself
# and the Old Curmudgeon

I doorstep him, whom I might have called my first love,
wonder what kind of old he is.

How will it look, brittle bones, sarcopenia?

A jacket as always too long in the sleeve
too big on the shoulder

a snow of dead cells.
I think of old times over

and over, his soul under a pile of newspapers
and pillars of books like the ones inside the hall door.

Philosophy, theology, human development, titles visible
definitions of pneuma in the fusty air,

the curtains closed day and night, I hear
the neighbours say, in all the high windows.

What is he doing time for, I wonder
as time is undoing him?

The air is still fresh out here
and two roses are helplessly beautiful

in the forecourt.

# Prospect Lane

A pretty wallpaper peels back to a red wall,
a scab torn to bleeding
where I had hoped for healing.

Amber haloes in the rain
the only cheer
as I walk back again over my last year

of red brick and divan
my life dripping through
drops in a hedgerow, like dew

hidden in the undergrowth
my fears of growing old
peering into other gardens, feeling cold.

# Walking with a Six-Year-Old in the Woods

She wants to know why girls begin with *g* boys with *b*?
I measure in the tunnels of my thought possible links, amuse myself
teasing, *guh*, 'girl' and *beh*, 'boy' against *guh*, 'good' and *beh*, 'bad'
by which time she's had another question.
I think of how questions hold onto us like ivy on trees, encircle our certainties.
I tell her we are trees, listening to the code of other leaves,
poplars trembling, sycamores swaying, willows swishing
in the mystery of the breeze, in each a purling through xylem and phloem,
carrying riffs of thrush, caw of crow into our core.

She wonders about sounds whose meaning we do not know.
We stretch our arms to the big sky, light and air, moving
through blue then grey, our ears straining for the littlest sigh,
every sound registered even before it has meaning, *Could you hear that leaf fall?*
she asks as we watch the first autumn leaves make their way to the ground.
Before I can answer she has found in a tangle of ivy
a magic home in a Cypress bole. *Please, please, can we play house?*

*Whose woods these are I think I know.* We sip rainwater tea
from big leaves and eat wildgrass cookies, and before we go, we hug
the rough unyielding bark to say thank you. *Can we come tomorrow
again? And the day after? And the day after?* she says
*And then the tree will know what we sound like and say hello!*

# Mating Mallards

A conference of pairs, they arrive over the weir,
ducks to water
squabbles of single sex everywhere.

It's February, a pet day
and they're assessing the air
like imams the moon.

They want to get a move on
the drakes have a job to do
to get their ducks in a row.

Suddenly one female is pinioned underwater
in a thug's embrace,
a contestable date rape,

yet they swim excitedly upstream
and back again, continue what seems
like the necessary imperatives

of some libidinous, salacious
exploitative dance.
I'm outraged for the females

but see quickly it's only water off a duck's back
as they shake themselves off
and calmly go back downstream.

# I Dream of a Bull Huss

A sudden tug and resistance at the end of my line
hysterical laughing as I pull in the best fish
thumping, escaping my grasp, his small head flailing,
a rush of ripples in his rub skin

which I know could leave me writhing and torn.
I let him off the hook and he strikes his pose,
shows off once more his contractile strength.
I slide him off-board and he bolts into the deep.

As I sleep that night in my old home
the bull huss becomes a floppy febrile fraidy-cat.
I fret about the boat
which might run aground in the muddy inlet.

I see through an isinglass lens a world blurred,
a mermaid's purse of worry stones burst
over auguries of mating
something yet to come from behind the rocks.

The witch Circe plunges the Bull Huss into the murk
turns him from nurse hound to nymph.
My headache's worse.
I can hear the wailing in the distance now,

a mermaid lost on the rocks
virgin on the ridiculous,
her hair tangled in the bladder wrack,
my own voice coming back to me.

*Four*

# Birthdays

*for Andrew and Philippe*

## I

I hold your lopping, exhausted head
and marvel at this flesh of my flesh
your soft skin, the fist of your little hand
up to your O so yawning mouth
as you relax up against me knowing already
that's where you should be, that you have arrived.
Outside I hear gulls and it is morning
in this seaside town where you are born
in this seaside town, in this hospital where
my father died and drew his last breath... Andrew...
and drew you to me on the breath of a new morning
this morning, where you are love come back
and I kiss your little forehead and name you
for the spirit of the ancestor in you, strong and true.

## II

Your presence felt before even the butterflies,
against the predictions of medics, science.
When you arrive just on the turn of the night
you are so alive you turn your eyes towards me
at the sound of my voice.
I hold you in my arms until morning
you and I, not yet separable.
You so born of desire that when I name you
for the sacred white horses of Herodotus
I am thinking of their beauty and their all-seeing eyes
as they move over the plains to bring new life
to you, and to me as you sparkle, breathe
their beauty wild and healing.
They are asking us to get ready for a long journey.

# Auguries

I was sad like a prophet last night, weary and heartbroken
about nothing I could figure out. And today the news comes
that it is your heart that is broken. You'll have stents.

Somewhere in my body I knew before the words were spoken
of the impending strife which moved around
looking for outlet, aggravating me.

The cardiac event is looking for its proper place
in a story of your own choosing. In your own voice
it doesn't matter how convoluted the plot is.

# Beetle

A ladybird without a spot, out on the pathway on a hot afternoon.
You speeding home over the drumlins, the familiar chug,
the last turn, nonchalantly acknowledged by the dog ready to wag his tail
as we run to the car to see all the goodies from Westport
in your cardboard box in the front seat, cheese in muslin and loose tea
white batch loaf and blackcurrant jam inspected in anticipation of the evening meal
and maybe there were iced caramels or emeralds, and if there were
we made sun-glasses, rings with the coloured plastic and foil in the haze
of early summers, dust on the road, the black outershell glossy in sunlight,
delicate though sturdy, the sacred scarab of resurrection and immortality there
in front of us, no house within a mile's radius, an engine's roar, no car
other than yours, with wings, god of invisible influences,
gentle messages whirring in the memory of your wonder machine
*koleos, koleos, koleoptera*

# Steering Wheel

I'm older than you were when you died.
Look at the fields, still the magical light,

your elbow on the open window, your imbibing green
as I do now, not just a colour or a feeling

but a lifestyle you'd be proud to be part of, Dad
who wanted us to name the milch cow.

Your old landmarks gone, a road carved out of the Rossduane
drumlin bypassing the bend to your old school,

the city, a maze of roundabouts. You never saw one
yet I imagine you'd love driving around them

and going onto motorways, to places you might have known
but would not know now, and *ghost estates* resurrected into *dormitory* towns.

Your Opel estate, pale blue with red leather seats, which I sat in for years
would be *hybrid* if you came back. I'd have to teach you *textspeak*

explain *Facebook* and *Twitter*, the weird virtual world as parallel to us
as the one you're in now.

I wish I could *Facetime* you and enter the *domain* of Dad.

You'd laugh at my *bling*, my efforts to *chillax*, the schoolmaster
of long ago would caution me for sloppy retorts like *whatever*

and quotatives flouting grammar as in, *I'm like, OMG!*
I dream of us meeting over a *wrap* (a sandwich) in the *bistro* (the pub).

You'd have tea strong enough for a mouse to trot on (you often said that)
and I'd have an almond milk *latté* (from far off Italy).

I'd tell you how I left for Philadelphia and studied a science not invented
in your time, but maybe it was you who sowed the seed

leafing through a rare sociology book explicating for me, expounding
social structure, and now decades of new words which you tossed into
    my young life

are *trending*, beating out a consciousness in borderlands
I hardly understand.

It doesn't matter because there is something stronger than words,
the memory of your hand

stretching out to the backseat as we drive along
I stretch out mine to where my sons sit as we weave our way

through childhood.
They ask me, *what was your Dad like?*

I tell them you're like the engine hiding in the bonnet,
we don't see it but we depend on it.

I hear them catching their imaginary steering wheels,
testing the pickup, excited, revving up, rearing to go.

# About a Heart and Its Ancestry

Two grandchildren at my father's grave
who have never met him, contemplating death,

afraid of it like one fears the depths
of the ocean on the shore.

I ask them what they are thinking
and their eyes fill with tears.

I hold them
helpless from grief, the wound of absence

over all those years felt again,
a growing pain in a new generation.

# Cabbage Butterfly

A cabbage butterfly en route home
distracted by broken clay and the smell, the flow

of blood-soaked clods in a dark rivulet
beside blonde hair on a girl's body stretched face down.

Not that the butterfly mourns the coming and going,
its wafer wings, its primrose powder pile

so delicate against the wind, against smudging
by alien things that it does well to live beyond a day,

and now, here it is after a summer.

It knows the difference between hurricanes and sirens,
alights for one delicate kiss on her still back, the alluring perfumes

of her hair and skin, tiny wafts which draw it in
but underneath in the lower notes something undesirable.

Tales of cabbages and what you might find
under them, not in the summer lore of its generation.

Or decay. How quickly it starts. The butterfly knows it is like a thought,
flits into space and breaks its flutter, checking in and out

of this world, like the fingertips of a girl which played out some tune
on a window sill, stumbled on the grace notes

as she waited for her lover.

# Rearview Mirror

I rise against you, trace my insurgence on the fogged-up glass.
Why have you got the steering wheel?

Your thoughts are far away from me, you use them to build a wall,
something I push against as I ask you why you are not talking.

You cannot say. No reason really. We pass through towns,
people we know waving in at us, but we sit in silence

the rearview mirror noting what will be left behind.

# Winter Storm at Coole

The wind rises suddenly outside Coole Park
shakes the car and me. The trees sway,
set free their limbs

and, grasping at the air
swirl in a macabre dance,
fall dangerously into my path.

The branches of ash
bleeding their red berries
flash and morph into STOP.

All I know of shelter torn
and thrown angrily by the elements.

Penelope realising Odysseus would not return for ages
cursing his boat to the mercy of easterlies.

The wipers beat out the uprooting methodically
as if to wipe my tears, swipe twigs off the windscreen,
violently soothe me.

Why did I come this road at all?
And now, can I see where it leads,
where I could possibly go?

My heart is lobbed onto my lap from the jolt
of sudden brakes, and then the road frees up,
someone else's doing...

I take my chance, speed off before a backup.

# The Pursuit of Happiness

Like Diarmuid and Gráinne
we drive westward across the country

on the M4, this navy road where we are zipped
into darkness, homeless, unsure.

We plough through the Bog of Allen,
along the flood plains of the Shannon

meander through Roscommon onto Newport,

orange cats eyes converging in the distance,
warnings from Benwisken still out of range.

The rain is falling pitter-patter over all of Ireland
pushing us back into this human cave

of a nineties Corolla, the wipers a metronome,

*kerplunk kerplunk*, which iterate our fears,
wipe away the whoosh of tears

as if that would help us see more clearly
our lives thrown into this vortex of road,

mortgage refusals behind the last door we closed.

Despite the Google maps, despite the promises
of better times ahead, our destiny unknown.

# The Night I Met Jesus on a Dublin Bike

Who is that man cycling on ahead
who looks back to check I'm keeping up
a little amused perhaps by my struggle
through the traffic.

All I know is that he has a heart,
the conclusion of little details,
how he remembers what I say
and holds my words like a shaman.

This is what I think as I spin
through the air from Blessington Basin
and down by Belvedere,
where we stop.

He bends down to put on
my visibility anklet
joking that now I'll be able to put
my best foot forward

as we go with the wind down the quays.
I'm too focused to notice
the distractions of the city
on the side.

At the lights he goes on ahead,
his visibility vest dazzling
and the light of his helmet
flickering like a sanctuary lamp.

Our destination, a pizzeria
where we sit and eat,
chat about where we've been
where we'll go from here.

*Five*

# Moment of Reckoning

Suddenly I did not belong to her story,
her eyes flitting with anger, mine not knowing

where best to look into the future,
aware that in this cast I had become

the grim reaper, the last flash of evening sun
on the sickle of my silver moon,

the darkness coming down between us.

# In the Beginning

We were one river of blood,
very excited ova settling into our luscious beds
and growing into sacks of happiness.

As tissue stretched, stabs of light announcing
our little death, down the wet exit,
left you out of breath from the backup,

the river running riot, bursting into places it ought not go,
not going where it should, and now all those red tributaries between us,
such a bloody tangle, a bloody mess.

I feel the bank of bone upon which you were dashed
hanging on the edge of cacophony, quiet in a cotton wool bassinet
as I slept on, truly delivered.

And what is really remembered?
These soft interiors, how we reached out
and found our little fingers,

others around and alarming whispers,
some hushed business
about the future.

# Twins, Still

In the garden, soil streams through his man hands in gaps of awkwardness
as we plant the future.

Sad and frustrated I try to decode
the raucous vowels of his misapprehension, the high pitch of his fears.

I think I am the unsealer of his soul, I want to fuse him to reality
rouse Endymion from his sleeping cave

but he lives without the symbols I know,
the Strawberry Moon swelling the sky above us, speaking to Saturn.

It seems to me that he believes in speleology,
divining by well rehearsed rituals the nature of things,

putting a jinx on what happens, offering gestures, mind games
to anchor us in the kitchen, wearing my apron as a ritual robe,

looking up to heaven before he places in the drain grid with apt reverence
the precious metals of the earth, a screw or tack.

He twirls before he goes back through the great doorways
of the house and visits the rooms of our living,

a stickler for ceremonies of feeding, rest, ablutions,
and when the music is playing between us, the exquisite pleasure

more beautiful than even I have words for,
as memories and feelings weave through a silence

like the ancient tides of amnion, the blood of our pulse
when the music is playing between us.

He has arrived like me as accurately as if a tuning fork had set his course,
pitch perfect, and to his delight, I come with an old refrain

making words in my mouth for him and spewing them, like molten gold
—*how loveliness increases and will never pass to nothingness*—
the little parable of our twinness, out.

# The Square in Front of the Archangels

It started with hopscotch, a stone and squares,
a way to pass the time waiting for your mother,

you, convinced you could put everything
into the neat categories they were once in

meticulously counting with your feet every square
on the cobble without trespassing a line,
without tripping into the tiny interstitial dykes.

You tested your balance on the diagonals,
hopped on every odd number, criss-crossed your legs

into the most restricted spaces, keeping your nerve
when you were out of breath, holding out on those fractals of fate

as you made your way, tippy-toe onto the smallest square
you imagined in the centre.

This is how you tested those inevitable consequences
as dark descended on the quiet waters of the mall,
the rooks about to startle from the Angelus bells

and become black angels from hell rising victorious
from the trees, distorting that square on which you landed

into a dark rectangle into which your father fell
while Michael, Raphael and Uriel were asleep.

# Angel

Gabriel from Hartford beside me
in this aircraft as we fly out of the mid-West,
Chicago now a memory.

Across from my hotel window
a nuclear family on the twenty fourth floor,
their lives unfolding like a spring flower,

their comings and goings
a cameo of civility. Like my life once,
my little son bopping between my husband and me

looking out on a puddle on a flat roof
in an apartment in Rosemont PA
saying *No cow!* mournfully.

Now I look out the porthole
back into my life,
the past picture perfect.

On the slow and considerate descent
I am comforted by Gabriel's earnest blue eyes.
I learn from him

that it is good what I do
and he tells me somewhat apologetically
when we go through turbulence

he has a fear of flying.
I have a fear of going nowhere.
I say nothing. He is too young to understand.

I don't know how to tell him
how bumping into him puts the aircraft, for now
back on course

and somehow on landing,
I'm ready for takeoff.

*Six*

# Chambers' Ice Cream

I take the train from Ogilvie to Palatine,
imagine her now at eighty three from my childhood
memory of nineteen seventy four. I go in and out of stations
like decades on a rosary and half-remembered licks of ice cream
to the day she was a queen with her king in her carriage, her retinue
Jo and I, princesses, as we wove our way through the mountains.

We thought the sun set like a red lollipop in the mountains
as Connemara glowed for us, imprinting this memory for Palatine
on this visit in two thousand and thirteen, the entire golden retinue
all her girls and boys, grown into lords and ladies from childhood.
*They still remember,* she laughs, *the taste of Chambers' ice cream
in Newport en route to Achill. That year we were there for the Stations...*

She takes out the Irish china, adjusts the radio stations
until she finds Irish music and melodies from the mountains
like home, serves up her apple pie with a dollop of ice cream
as she tells me who's schizophrenic, gay, divorced in Palatine.
And how she became a nurse, the dream of her childhood.
When she went back to school, she showed this gifted retinue

where their brains came from! Did I mention the genuine beauty of her retinue?
I see their high cheekbones and auburn hair in photos above the play station
which detail their rights of passage and moments of glory from childhood.
They were paraded every few years, money permitting, in the Achill mountains,
a far and distant cry from this conurbation in Illinois, Palatine
the place where they romped their way through childhood.

*We made sure our little yanks had a chance to see our childhood,
the goats and sheep which in those days, their father teased, were my retinue!
Hard to imagine, she said, around these red brick condos of Palatine...
We made them do the climb on Croagh Patrick up to the first station
harder than the steps in the Wrigley Building, a mountain of mountains
for little feet, she smiled. redeemed at the bottom by Chambers' ice cream.*

Ireland, for them a blissful world, everywhere there were lollipops and ice cream
melting between wafers, like the two continents of their childhood,
and when life was hard they knew a path in the mountains,
and nostalgic, tried out orienteering at home later in Palatine,
grew up fast, and now their children rise to her station,
the little ones who come for consolation to the Nurse of Palatine.

She says, *You are the new generation, the golden retinue
of your Gran. Enjoy childhood, eat ice cream as you move from station to station.
This is what sustained us from the Achill mountains to Palatine!*

# Penelope

Penny lives here with the kids
and Ods is in London
fighting all kinds of battles, she says,
on the Stock Exchange.

She takes it in her stride
the way her mother before her did
when her father emigrated
to tatiehoke in Scotland.

No use looking out wistfully from the
Atlantic Drive or Achill head,
her Dad was bent over a dark ridge
somewhere north of Aberdeen.

She didn't even know. He was gone
and she got on with it,
got used to saying he was away,
wondered what he was like on long winter nights

when her mother sat by the fire
and knitted Aran sweaters for the factory.
Each wondered but would never ask
if he'd ever get back.
It wasn't as if no one cared.

Now she knows the wisdom
of not saying it as it is
even with Skype and Instagram
she knows how it feels,

absence like the empty side of the bed
and the silence of the late evening
when the children are asleep
the way the dog looks at the front door

and she sees her mother darning reason
into feelings she couldn't mend,
even if it was love that made the stitches
she'd still throw it from her in the end
say, *There it is now, that'll do.*

# Look at the Flowers of the Field

Cobalt gentians at Eagle's Rock with their startling white eyes
and out across the Burren, orchid spikes
of pink and white, and bird's-foot trefoil and burnet rose
and the common violet and all that grows
softly moving in the low breeze close to the ground
in among rock and grass as dry as desert scutch.
You are asking yourself what compels you as such,
you, with your great consciousness compared to theirs
hacking out survival in the hardest layers
of rock, what is it you need of their perfection and fragility?
As you gaze on the delicate petals, a certain equanimity
comes, leaves you searching still for what precisely occurs
in you as you flit over the velvet blue, satin yellow, pink and white lace,
and burst for their beauty, resilience, grace.

# Grief is a Thing with Feathers

a black crow which sits on the garden wall
when the news comes

a robin which flies into the house like a harbinger
of healing, weeks later.

Months on, an egret stabs at something good in seaweed
at dusk, some food for the night,

a healing which you imagine might come in due course
if you have heart enough to wait in the shadows.

# No, I Cannot Go Home, I Don't Know
# What to Say to the Children

We drive through the housing estates of South Dublin,
flowering trees sodden with tears.

I imagine pristine lives unstained by words such as I would have to utter
so we drive for over an hour

until the rain stops or the flood recedes, or whatever it was that opened
a path back to our house. I turn the key

and go quietly in from the night,
the baby still holding court in his chair
until he sees me, wants to be picked up.

My older son, flitting his dark eyes
to finds words, then asks what
we brought home for him.

The babysitter hurries away, says *we'll talk tomorrow*
and now it's snacks and stories and hugs,
no ugly words are spoken, and when they are tucked

the memory of the doctor crestfallen
delivering this news to the young woman
of thirty three, who is me.

The soft breathing of my sleeping children
rises and falls in the silence as I lie awake
not knowing what to say.

# I Think My Breasts Sing

*after Sharon Olds*

I want to burst forth, I tell you playfully,
like a soprano in counterpoint to your tantric thrum.
There they sit, my breasts, soft and heavy, gauche yet supple
enough to make the shape of our closeness,
propped by my ribcage on your chest
nonchalantly at rest like dotted minims.

I like that their whites are bigger than your eyes,
rounder than your open mouth,
and they dance as they shout, topple left and right
deflected by your Coriolis breath
and, amplified, prepare for the great moment
as their stippled centres rise like sentries.

When you take them, you, the great conductor, and spin them
like your two favourite singles onto the old turntable,
we are transported into the Milky Way like old times
and there they are, luminous like ageless stars
and I forget the lack of symmetry
and the silicone fillet sewn in

to the one near my heart. It has no voice
but if it had it would be creaking and cracking with sorrow
except for the way that you gather it into your hand
into a cup of victory, tell me how you love my history
and then I hear the soft baseline beat of my heart.

# The Hammam

Water flows over my body, bashful at first
by its exposure to light and water and then

as if I were the stones of a waterfall
warm in winter sun, I bask in the flow

of its idle trickling between scrubbings,

the black soap like a pocked stone
picked up by a large naked woman

astride my thigh to find her angle
to work into my crevices and folds

as if they were the mossy mounds on the river bank

and not the obstinate bumps of flesh
I would not reveal at home.

I am loved in this space
where a young girl scrubs up her grandmother

and a nubile teenager sends the gift of shampoo
up a sudsy river.

Back in the city of robes they walk to their chores
in the souk, their deep eyes, their hands shine

from the loving touch here where water flows
in kind ablutions,

the sacred pourings to stop the thickening of skin,
the gnarling of their knuckles and joints

and to rinse their eyes, the blurring of the world for one minute
as it flows over them, and me.

I see solidarity is like this,
our voices no longer bitter, hoarse.

# Looking Like Rain

The bleaching of gorse at the end of spring,
the skin of your abdomen after winter,

the bleeding you never mentioned
until now, admitting you are actually consoled

by the confirmation of symptoms, relieved you say
with a certain exhilaration, but the word

the declaration of the state of affairs, unutterable,
its insinuation in every sentence of conversation

making new turns on old words
which were once innocuous, *manage, guarded, outlook,*

a sinister game of scrabble, with shifts and hedges,
the concessions of *palliative*, the ll's curling softly

rolling like acorns which have found themselves in the river
unexpectedly and are racing to the sea.

# À Plus

*"Vienne la nuit sonne l'heure*
*Les jours s'en vont je demeure"*
GUILLAUME APOLLINAIRE

i.m. Karine Chamaillard 1969-2011


You loved light and how to measure its mysteries,
tried to explain to me the vectors of its possibility,
its scattering in our daily lives,

how refraction and diffusion,
the variance of waves, makes our lives beautiful,
gives us blue sky, crepuscular rays.

But you had no instrument to explain
the flashes of confusion
in your own mind at its flickering

or why in the end
you were following
some rough interstellar grain.

You wanted to go home
to settle into old memories,
assuage the pain. It was the look in your eye

the last time we sat for lunch à la *Defense*,
where you roller-skated as a child in the shadows of skyscrapers.
We visited all your old haunts

then said goodbye on a bridge in Paris at nightfall,
away in different directions, polarised particles
back to where we came from.

# She Lives Everyday as if it Were Her First

*for Helen Donoghue*

She has just discovered the beauty of *Sole Mio,*
trips with delight on every emotional contour.

She's all *iTunes* and *YouTube* this evening, asks me to dance
to Handel's *Did You Not Hear My Lady?*

We waltz out the four-four with little steps
down the corridor of the nursing home, laughing like old times.

She looks at me lovingly and says
*You are a beautiful person.*

*Where did we first meet?*
*You remind me of someone I know.* I see she's intrigued.

*Aah, you deserve only the best darling,* she says
pirouetting and proffering her wedding ring

engraved 1969. She talks of the place
where Dad gave it to her, the old music stand

in Dún Laoghaire Harbour. I hear seagulls and ship horns
in her quaking voice.

She's still with Handel and tries to sing
*Beyond My Open Window,* stumbles on *restless wings.*

By bedtime there is no song left in her. She's breathless,
frets over buttons which won't close

knows that it's a hairbrush in her hand
but cannot brush her hair.

Suddenly on the edge, she's lucid and terrified
there's nothing to gather up, remember after the day.

I hold her hand, stroke its veined maps,
places too I've been,

impossible to save her from the detonation
of time bombs after plaques and tangles in her brain.

I put my arms around her and try not to weep, the daughter
who is singing lullabies to put her mother to sleep

*Golden slumbers kiss your eyes… smiles await you when you rise*
*Hush little baby don't you cry…*

I try to stay in the moment,
hold her like my child
as the hours, the days, slip by.

# As She Died

A tear sat on the sill of her eye
like a young girl on a fence in summer
dangling her legs, wondering what she would do next

some eighty years before.
In this moment the blue of her eye more intense
than it had ever been, and now about to close.

The lid came down like an old curtain
made from crimped flour bags
(as in the old days) and I imagined it as Venus

in the eastern sky heading up as the sun goes down
spinning homewards to a constellation
where her other eye had already turned.

The day after she was buried
it poured. I thought about her boat
the one she told me about a day or two before.

She said that maybe she was going
under, looked me in the eye
to see if I understood.

Now the flood is rising
and rocking her from this side.

Her eyes closed, she clutches the oars
up on her chest like a prayer,

an incantation. Behind the glabella
the silence of eternity,

the still point
I imagine beyond

the rhythm of rain, disturbed air.

# Family Funeral

We rarely meet now
except to bury the dead
and our hatchets for the day
as we stand saluting those who no longer have to survive
the hypocrisies of backbiting, short-sightedness, lies.
Hardly surprising the family funeral is sad,
the helpless handshakes wishing it otherwise,
not knowing how one might rise above
the petty inheritances poorly understood from childhood,
prejudices before opinions were made,
thin tears tipping off eyelids as we try to fathom
how blood is thicker than water,
and when the goodbyes are spoken
the cruel irony of knowing – already–
when we will meet again.

# Kylemore Abbey – A Valediction Forbidding Mourning

The moon streams blue through a turret, behind which I hear voices,
the *Dames d'Ypres* calling me, *"Venez, venez ici!"*
Every time I cut a corner they are gone to the next one,
the soft hum of Vespers echoing down the corridors
to the Front Hall where I first heard the haunt

of Gregorian chant one summer's evening after the war.
Paper-thin the swish of serge robes on the cold floors
as the Dames line up in the choir, not like black crows
but like swallows on a wire, waiting for the right moment.
My eyes look North from the balustrade.

Rows of short headstones, blue teeth
with one gap, thirty railings in as you count East
on the metal fence. (Where I'll be). The storm gathers
as the sisters encircle me, psalters in hand, their old vocal chords join notes
to words, *Receive her soul…*Then, I hear the heavy door clang.

I am wearing the black habit I made for this journey
when I was a novice, its heavy folds crimped to the neck
but now somehow airily light. I am inside every room racing
at my heart's pace through corridor and portal. Where I once lived.
I do not need that blue moon to see where I am going.

# Amphitrite at Achill Head

I watch her rise in this Achill woman's eyes,
something homey and fragile about her
as she sips opposite me, as if her tea were full of essential plankton,
as if her bulging eyes were the result of hard earned insights.

I see her survey the sound, imagine her out there,
her hair in tresses, gathered in a net, the colour of yellow flag iris.
Once she was slender and exquisite as a birch tree,
now she is heavy and beaten by south westerlies.

Often she skipped along the road in Kildavnet,
tells me as she remembers it, smiles, clear as she does
what she once was. She doesn't tell me about Dympna
or why she died.

Her fish eyes scan Achill head,
the thick though tender lips of her cavernous mouth
open and close for sips of the sea. She knows how to live there,
proceeds unperturbed through her playground,

her tail and fins at work, goes gently into unfamiliar territory,
makes deep forays into places no one else would go
as she weaves her old ways through the current,
and when she sets out to the deep

she trembles with love for the silver shoals
released beyond the tombolo, her heart wrenched
from what she knows as she watches them with envy and resignation
rise like foals from the spray
released to the world,
galloping to that destiny ahead of them.

# Egrets on the Flaggy Shore

The stunning white backs
against the dark wrack
of the foreshore.

The delicate studied steps
as they pick through the depths
down to the rocks

exotic and strange, this dash of white
on the darks and greys in the fading light
of an Irish winter

as beautiful as a Syrian
after rain,
her skin golden, glistening

as beautiful as an erratic in the wall
fitting there like a cornerstone,
knowing this place can be its home.

# Acknowledgments

Grateful acknowledgement is made to the editors of the following journals and publications in which some of these poems first appeared, sometimes in slightly different forms: *Stand, The Interpreter's House, The Irish Times, Headstuff.org, Southward, Crannóg, The Galway Review, and, Open-Eyed, Full-Throated, An Anthology of American/Irish Poets* (Arlen House, 2019), *Reading the Future, New Writing from Ireland* (Arlen House 2018), *Washing Windows? Irish Women Write Poetry* (Arlen House, 2016), *Even The Daybreak: 35 Years of Salmon Poetry* (Salmon, 2016) and *The Poet's Quest for God* (Eyewear, 2016).

My thanks also to those who supported my writing in other practical ways over the last few years: Nat Anderson (Arts Representative), Heather Corbally Bryant, Christine Casson, Renny Golden, Kathryn Kirkpatrick, David Lloyd, Ann Nealon, Thomas O'Grady, Dan Tobin, Eamonn and Drucilla Wall (The American Conference for Irish Studies); Joseph Lennon, Jennifer Joyce, MaryLu Hill (Villanova University); Mary Burke and Lisa Taylor (University of Connecticut), Lorna Shaughnessy, Rachel Coventry, Emily Cullen, Connie Masterson, Tom Lavelle and Aideen Henry (Workshop); The Pen2Paper,Heart2Page collective, Christine O'Dowd Smyth (WIT) and Maureen Ruprecht Fadem(CUNY) for regular engaging and stimulating conversations about poetry, among other things, Brendan Duddy SJ (former poetry editor of Studies) for reading earlier versions of several of these poems and offering most helpful feedback; The Bosom Pals Project (Ruth Cadden, Marion Cox, Mary Hanlon, Susan Lindsay, Mari Maxwell, Robyn Rowland, Lorna Shaughnessy and Jennifer Skeffington (admin); Strokestown International Poetry Festival 2018 and Clifden Arts Festival 2018; The Capturing Granuaile Project curated by Sarah Kelly McCabe. Also Rosaleen Heraty, Westport Townhall.

For invitations to read: Kevin Higgins and Susan Millar Dumars (Over the Edge, Galway), Kate Ennals (At The Edge, Cavan), Isabelle Torrance (University of Notre Dame and now Aarhus Institute of Advanced Studies), Jack Harte and Saïd Tigraoui, Festival International de Poésie, Marrakech (Spring, 2017), Paul Casey (Ó Bhéal Readings, Cork, May 2017), Michael O'Sullivan (Chinese University of Hong Kong, 2018), Barbara McKeown (Cuckoo Festival, Kinvara), David Green (Off The Page, Athenry), Double Shot, Books Upstairs (2015) and Sunday Sessions, Books Upstairs (2018), and Larry Robin (Moonstone, Philadelphia, 2019).

For media interviews: Ryan Tubridy, RTÉ Radio 1 (Morning Show, 1st March, 2017), Keith Finnegan, Galway Bay FM (Morning Show,15th September, 2017) Tommy Marren, Midwest Radio (14th February, 2017), Karen McDonnell, Kinvara FM (4th November, 2017) and Eileen Keane, Clifden Radio (7th December, 2017).

For reviews: Joseph Horgan (*Burning Bush II*), Rachel Bower (*Stand*) Kevin Higgins (*The Galway Advertiser*).

I am especially indebted to Medbh McGuckian for her kind endorsement of my work. As always, my thanks to James Harrold (Arts Officer, Galway) for his constant interest and support.

My thanks to Breda Burns who created the beautiful painting of the egret, to Siobhán Hutson of Salmon Poetry for all the design work, and to my neighbour and Fine Arts photographer Markus Voetter for the portrait photo.

My deepest gratitude to my two sons, Andrew and Philippe Madec, for their constant love and support of all my work, and to Conall O'Cuinn, my husband, for his undying interest in me and poetry. His wit and good humour keep me going even when the clouds hang low.

Finally my thanks to Jessie Lendennie for believing in my work and supporting me in the family of the Salmon authors.

MARY MADEC received her M.A. in Old English poetry from NUI, Galway and her doctorate in Linguistics from the University of Pennsylvania. She is currently Director of the Villanova Study Abroad Program at NUI, Galway. She won the Hennessy XO Prize for Emerging Poetry in 2008. Her first collection, *In Other Words*, was published by Salmon Poetry in 2010 followed by *Demeter Does Not Remember* in 2014. She also edited *Jessica Casey & Other Stories* from Salmon Poetry, 2011, showcasing work from people with intellectual disabilities following a multi-award winning project funded by an Arts Participation Bursary from the Arts Council of Ireland. Recently she has worked with immigrant writers. She is also a member of a collective of poets who, through poetry readings, reach to women who have had breast cancer and a co-author of their book *Bosom Pals* published by Doire Press in 2017.

# salmonpoetry

Cliffs of Moher, County Clare, Ireland

"Like the sea-run Steelhead salmon that thrashes upstream to its spawning ground, then instead of dying, returns to the sea—Salmon Poetry Press brings precious cargo to both Ireland and America in the poetry it publishes, then carries that select work to its readership against incalculable odds."

TESS GALLAGHER

# The Salmon Bookshop
# & Literary Centre

Ennistymon, County Clare, Ireland